SHORT HISTORY OF THE LONDON RIFLE BRIGADE

SHORT HISTORY

OF THE

LONDON RIFLE BRIGADE

Compiled Regimentally

ALDERSHOT:
PRINTED BY GALE & POLDEN LTD.,
WELLINGTON WORKS.

1916.

Frontispiece.

Photo: Underwood & Underwood.

LT.-COL. N. C. KING, T.D., Comdg. 3rd Battn.

LT.-COL. G. R. TOD, Comdg. 2nd Battn.

LT.-COL. A. S. BATES, D.S.O., Comdg. 1st Battn.

NOTE

Pending the full pre-war history, which is to be written by better hands, the very sketchy outline in Part I. is given in order to form the connecting link between the Regiment in peace, since its formation, and the present time.

It does not attempt to give the smallest idea of the hard work, often accomplished under disadvantageous circumstances, carried out by all ranks, which made possible the work done in the war.

That the Regiment even now exists is solely due to Lieut.-Colonel Lord Bingham (now Brigadier-General the Earl of Lucan), whose cheery optimism through the dark times previous to the birth of the Territorial Force was such a great tower of strength.

Any profits which may accrue from this pamphlet will be given to the London Rifle Brigade Prisoners' Aid Fund.

October, 1916.

CONTENTS

	PAGE
Part I	1
Part II	7
Second Battalion	30
Third Battalion	31
Administrative Centre	33
Appendix A	35
Appendix B	39
Appendix C	40
Appendix D	45
Appendix E	46
Appendix F	47

SHORT HISTORY
OF THE
LONDON RIFLE BRIGADE

PART I.

The London Rifle Brigade, formerly the 1st **Formation.** London Volunteer Rifle Corps (City of London Rifle Volunteer Brigade), and now, officially, the 5th (City of London) Battalion The London Regiment, London Rifle Brigade, familiarly known to its members and the public generally by the sub-title or the abbreviation "L.R.B.," was founded July 23rd, 1859, at a meeting convened by the Lord Mayor. It has always been intimately associated with the City of London, its companies being under the patronage of the various Wards.

Within a week of its formation the muster of the Regiment exceeded 1,800; two battalions were formed and headquarters were taken at No. 8, Great Winchester Street, where they remained for 34 years, and subsequently in Finsbury Pavement.

In 1893 the Regiment entered its present headquarters in Bunhill Row. These were designed by the late Lieut.-Colonel Boyes, erected entirely from regimental funds, supplemented by contributions from members of the Brigade, from various City Companies and other friends of the Regiment, and constitute the finest building of its kind in London.

Since the formation of the Territorial Force these headquarters have been shared with the Post Office Rifles.

Honorary Colonel. Mr. Alderman Carter was at first appointed Honorary Colonel, but in 1860 it was suggested that a military Honorary Colonel would be more appropriate than a civilian one, and Mr. Carter (then Lord Mayor) approached H.R.H. the Duke of Cambridge, who in response to the unanimous wish of the Regiment, accepted the appointment, which he held until his death in 1904. During this period he rarely missed attending the annual inspection.

Commanding Officers In 1862 a resolution was passed at a meeting " that Regimental Commanding Officers should now and always be Officers of professional experience and ability." This tradition has been departed from on only two occasions prior to the war, as shown in the list given on the following page.

Name.	From.	To.
G. M. Hicks (late 41st Regiment)	30/12/59	January, 1862.
G. Warde (late 51st Regiment)	February, 1862	Early, 1876.
Sir A. D. Hayter, Bt. (late Grenadier Guards)	Early, 1876	1881.
W. H. Haywood (Ex London Rifle Brigade)	1881	1882.
Lord Edward Pelham-Clinton (late Rifle Brigade)	June, 1882	1890.
H. C. Cholmondeley (late Rifle Brigade)	1890	February, 1901.
Edward Matthey (Ex London Rifle Brigade)	February, 1901	4/6/01.
Lord Bingham (late Rifle Brigade)	June, 1901	1913.
Earl Cairns (late Rifle Brigade)	1913	1915.
Norman C. King (Ex London Rifle Brigade)	1915	

1st Battalion.

Earl Cairns	4/8/14	16/3/15.
A. S. Bates (Ex London Rifle Brigade)	16/3/15	15/8/16.
R. H. Husey (Ex London Rifle Brigade)	15/8/16	

2nd Battalion.

G. R. Tod (late Seaforth Highlanders)	September, 1914	

3rd Battalion.

B H. C. Cholmondeley	30/11/14	1915.
2 Norman C. King	4/6/15	

South African War.

Colonel Cholmondeley was appointed to command the Mounted Infantry Section of the C.I.V., to which regiment the London Rifle Brigade contributed 2 officers (Captain C. G. R. Matthey and Lieutenant the Hon. Schomberg K. McDonnell) and 78 other ranks.

When the Volunteer Active Service Companies were raised, 17 members were accepted for service with the Royal Fusiliers, and an additional 76 joined the Imperial Yeomanry and R.A.M.C.

The total death roll of the Regiment was seven.

Colonel Cholmondeley, Lieutenant E. D. Johnson (Imperial Yeomanry), and Colour-Sergeant T. G. Beeton (C.I.V. Infantry) were mentioned in despatches.

Honours.

Colonel holmondeley received the C.B. for his services in South Africa, and Lieutenant the Hon. Rupert Guinness was made a C.M.G. for his work with the Irish Hospital.

When the Coronation honours were announced in 1902, Colonel Edward Matthey, V.D., received the C.B., a fitting award for his long services to the Volunteer Force. Before joining the L.R.B. in 1873 as a private he had already been 13 years in the Victoria Rifles. He retired in 1901, having served in every rank. His interest in the Regiment has been, and still is, without limit.

The work he has done for its welfare, while

THE CONVENT.
8th to 16th November, 1914.

PLOEGSTEERT.
The Brewery—The Battalion's First Bath house.

still serving, and since retirement, cannot be chronicled here, but, when the full history of the Regiment is written, Colonel Matthey's name will be found writ large on its pages.

In January, 1905, the Regiment was given the right to bear upon its "Colours and appointments" the words "South Africa, 1900-1902." **Battle Honours.**

The London Rifle Brigade has always been distinguished as a shooting regiment. In the very first year of its existence its co-operation was sought in connection with the formation of the National Rifle Association. In 1907 it had no less than a dozen International marksmen in its ranks. **Shooting.**

The earliest notable individual success was that of Private J. Wyatt, who won the Queen's Prize in 1864.

On two more occasions has the Blue Riband of the shooting world been won by members of the Regiment—in 1902 by Lieutenant E. D. Johnson, and in 1909 by Corporal H. G. Burr.

Regimental teams have been very successful both at the National Rifle Association and the London district meetings. At the latter the "Daily Telegraph" Cup was won two years in succession (1897 and 1898).

This was second to none in the Territorial Force. Its Annual Assault-at-Arms provided as stirring a spectacle as could be witnessed anywhere. For many years past the Brigade achieved notable successes at the Royal Military **School of Arms.**

Tournament and in the competitions of the Metropolitan Territorial School of Arms Association.

Athletics. The Battalion always took part in the various contests between the Territorial Regiments with considerable success. The most notable of late were the following:—The "Marathon" Race in the Territorial Championship of the London District, 1913, when Captain Husey and the London Rifle Brigade team won it in the record time of 1 hr. 33 min. 37 sec.; the distance was 12 miles, from Ewell to Stamford Bridge. The national contest at Newport did not produce such a good time, the London Rifle Brigade team winning it in 1 hr. 48 min. 14 sec.

The march to Brighton of 52½ miles for a team of sixty of all ranks, in full marching order, was accomplished in 1914 by a London Rifle Brigade team, under Captain Husey and Lieutenant Large, in the record time of 14 hrs. 23 min. The war has not given any other battalion a chance to lower the latter record, and it will assuredly take " some doing."

PART II.

The Battalion mobilised on the outbreak of **Mobilisa-** war. It had actually gone into camp at East- **tion.** bourne, but was brought back to London within a few hours of its arrival.

A second and third Battalion were soon formed. (See pp. 30, 31.)

FIRST BATTALION.

Making stays of varying duration en route at Wimbledon, Hersham, and Bisley (for three weeks), the 1st Battalion finally reached Crowborough, where it remained under canvas until ordered abroad.

It embarked on November 4th, 1914. The following were the officers:—

Lieut.-Col. W. D. Earl Cairns (Commanding).
Lieut.-Col. (Hon. Col.) C. G. R. Matthey, V.D. (Second-in-Command).
Major.—N. C. King, T.D.
Captains.—A. S. Bates, M. H. Soames, R. H. Husey, C. H. F. Thompson, H. F. MacGeagh, J. R. Somers-Smith, A. L. Lintott, and Hon. Major C. D. Burnell.
Lieutenants.—R. E. Otter, J. G. Robinson, G. H. Morrison, E. L. Large, P. A. Slessor, H. B. Price, A. G. Kirby, G. H. Cholmeley.

Second-Lieutenants.—K. Forbes, G. H. G. M. Cartwright, W. L. Willett, H. L. Johnston, C. W. Trevelyan, H. G. Vincent, G. E. S. Fursdon, G. C. Kitchin.
Adjutant.—Captain A. C. Oppenheim, K.R.R.C.
Quartermaster.—Lieutenant J. R S. Petersen.
Medical Officer.—Major A. D. Ducat, T.D.

The following short account is written in constant remembrance of the censorship regulations, and with a view to giving a faint outline of its doings to those who were not out with the 1st Battalion in France. It will be an aid to memory to those who were with it, and are fortunate in being able to look back on a time when the 1st Battalion undoubtedly reached its zenith.

Never can any Battalion of the Regiment be better than was the 1st London Rifle Brigade in 1914-15. That all will endeavour to be as good is quite certain.

1914. Nov. 5th. The Battalion arrived in France. Disembarkation was a tedious business, and the progress through the town to the rest camp at the top of the hill was one of the worst forms of route march the Battalion had ever experienced. Frequent checks, but no halts, taught the true weight of packs and kit; and a perfunctory inspection on arrival at the camp completed the exhaustion.

For the next three weeks the history of the Battalion was one common to those Territorial units which were sent out as lone Battalions about that time. It comprised a glorious uncertainty, which troops coming out earlier and later in complete divisions cannot have experienced. For instance, on landing it was learnt, quite by accident, but on excellent authority, that officers no longer wore Sam Browne belts or carried swords. A frantic rush at the last moment procured web equipment just before the parade to entrain. Swords and belts were left at the base.

There was much to learn about entrainment in France. An advance party had been sent forward some two hours earlier, and the rest of the Battalion and the transport were at the station by 4 p.m. The train was not due to leave until 9 p.m. French trains and the French railway system became familiar later on in all their ramifications, but at first "Hommes 40 Chevaux (en long) 8" aroused suspicions that were only too well justified in the next $21\frac{1}{2}$ hours before the train reached its destination. The experience was not a unique one. *Nov. 6th.*

On arrival at General Headquarters it was found that the Battalion was not even expected, and no arrangements had been made for the night. After a wait of three hours in the train, the Battalion moved off into some old artillery barracks, which were destined to become more familiar later on. The quarters were, at that time, about as dismal and dirty as can be imagined. *Nov. 7th.*

Nov. 8th. The Battalion marched out some three and a half miles to a large unfurnished and unfinished convent, which accommodated the entire strength.

There was no water laid on, no light, no method of heating or of drying clothes, no furniture, and no possibility of supplementing rations. The only bright spot was the first introduction to the rum ration.

Training, which consisted chiefly of trench digging and artillery formation, was carried out daily regardless of the weather.

The Battalion was apparently considered to be up to the required standard of efficiency and hardness, or else the authorities had not the heart to keep it there longer, for on the 15th orders were received to march the next day.

Nov. 16th. The distance was 17½ miles, and the roads *pavée* almost the whole way. There was also some rain. In spite, however, of the absence of other Battalions to keep them on their mettle, not a single man fell out of the column.

Nov. 17th. Except for bruised feet, the march next day, about 11 miles, was not very trying. Two nights were spent at this town, where the Artists and Honourable Artillery Company were also in billets.

While on the march it had been possible, for the first time, to see aeroplanes being shelled, and, while in these billets, the Battalion learnt what it meant to see the remnants of a Brigade come out of action.

The Battalion moved one stage nearer to the firing line in a snow-storm. **Nov. 19th.**

Brigadier-General Hunter Weston paid the Battalion a visit, and addressed the Officers. He gave a short account of the 11th Infantry Brigade, which he commanded, and to which the London Rifle Brigade was attached, and outlined the scheme of training. Half-companies were to be attached to Regular Battalions for a spell in the trenches, the men being scattered amongst the Regulars. As soon as their worth had been proved, half-companies were to be put in the line intact, and later whole companies. **Nov. 20th.**

At dusk on this date half the Battalion proceeded viâ Ploegsteert to the trenches.

For some unknown reason the Battalion had not been permitted to adopt the "double company system" in England, but on this date the change was made with half the Battalion absent in the trenches. **Nov. 21st.**

"A" and "D" Companies became No. 1, under Major King.

"E" and "O" Companies became No. 2, under Captain Soames.

"G" and "P" Companies became No. 3, under Major Burnell.

"H" and "Q" Companies became No. 4, under Captain Bates.

For the purposes of reference, these companies will be referred to as A, B, C, and D respectively, though, owing to the confusion that might have arisen with the old letters, this nomenclature was not actually adopted till after the second battle of Ypres.

Up to December 18th the trench training of the London Rifle Brigade continued. Platoons and whole companies, gradually working more and more on their own, were attached to the Regulars. When not actually in the line, the whole day was invariably taken up with "fatigues" of all kinds.

A support line in the wood was remade and named Bunhill Row.

It was during this period that the Battalion gained the nicknames "London fatigue party" or "Fatigue Fifth," and other affectionate titles which would not look well in print.

The Battalion also learnt what it meant to have the "dripping swung on it."

The 11th Infantry Brigade was composed of the following Battalions:—

  1st Somerset Light Infantry.
  1st East Lancashire Regiment.
  1st Hampshire Regiment.
  1st Rifle Brigade.

Dec. 19th. The object of the attack by the 11th Infantry Brigade in front of Ploegsteert Wood on this date was to clear its edges, including German

To face page 12.

PLOEGSTEERT.
Experimenting with a Rifle Grenade.
From Left to Right:—LIEUT.-COL. EARL CAIRNS, C.M.G., COL.-SGT. OVER.
STAFF-SGT. (NOW REGTL. SGT.-MAJ.) ADAMS, AND CAPT. OPPENHEIM, D.S.O.

To face page 13.

PLOEGSTEERT WOOD.

House, and, if possible, establish a line in front in the part afterwards known as the "birdcage."

The Somerset Light Infantry and Rifle Brigade attacked. The London Rifle Brigade was in support. The weather could not have been worse, and the ground was impossible. The result was that the wood was cleared, and German House remained in No Man's Land.

The London Rifle Brigade was not called upon to continue the attack. This was the first experience the Battalion had of anything like heavy artillery fire, and also of the difficulty of consolidating at night in an unknown bit of ground. Two half-companies were engaged in assisting in this work, while the rest of the Battalion spent a miserable night in the marshes in the wood.

Each of the four companies was definitely **Dec. 23rd.** attached, as a fifth company, to one of the Regular Battalions—" A " to the East Lancs, " B " to the Somerset Light Infantry, " C " to the Hants, and " D " to the Rifle Brigade.

All four companies of the London Rifle Brigade being in the front line on the same night, it so happened that before the end of 1914 a Territorial Battalion held the whole of a Regular Brigade's front with the exception of half a company on the extreme left.

The London Rifle Brigade was taken out of **1915.** the trenches preparatory to taking over a bit of **Jan. 5th.** line of its own on the right of the 11th Brigade.

Owing to the incursions of the river Warnave, this trench was in a very poor state of repair and badly flooded.

The dispositions of the Battalion were—one company in the front trench, one in London Farm and its environs (this supplied the night-carrying and working parties), one company, which was used for general fatigues for the Brigade, in reserve in Ploegsteert, and one company resting, washing, and cleaning in billets at Armentières. Every company spent three days in each place, and in many ways this was the most comfortable tour of duty the Battalion ever had.

The men made themselves thoroughly at home in the cottages of the village, while the three days' rest in Armentières owed much of its enjoyment to the initiative shown by the 4th Division in organising both divisional baths and divisional Follies.

Headquarters and various details, which included for the first time a permanent working and wiring party, were, of course, always "in action" in Ploegsteert.

Mar. 11th—20th. This was a period of "standing by" and various small moves, but eventually, after three days in the East Lancashires' trenches in front of the Convent, the Battalion took over the centre section in the wood on the 21st March.

Lieut.-Colonel Earl Cairns, C.M.G., owing to ill-health, left the Battalion on March 16th, and Major A. S. Bates took over command.

The section was held with three companies in the wood, and the fourth in reserve in the village. The other battalions of the 11th Brigade went into rest on the 16th, and the London Rifle Brigade came out last on the next day. The 11th Infantry Brigade was relieved by a brigade of the South Midland Division.

Mar. 21st— Apl. 17th.

The following extract from a letter shows the change of conditions between the first and second sojourn of the Battalion in the wood:—

"We are back again in the wood, and really almost glad, though I expect you will hardly believe it. Our quota of work in the winter no doubt did a good deal towards the transformation, and spring is now helping matters. The couduroy no longer stops at the worst parts, where we used to hold our breaths and make a dive for it. Hunter Avenue, and right beyond it to the end of the wood, is now quite a pleasant walk. Rations and carrying parties, though they have developed a rather peculiar gait, can progress at a reasonable pace, and have no need to wade so long as they keep to the boards. On either side, however, we still have a reminder of the nightmare that is past. The possibility of getting material up has a corresponding effect on the work in the trenches. The trench we were in on December 9th, which we could not conceive ever being anything but a drain, has now found its proper use. It has a new C.T. behind, and breastworks pushed out in front into the hedge, with little bridges across to each; so that altogether everything in the garden is as near lovely as can be."

The Bishop of London, the Senior Chaplain to the Regiment, during his visit to the front, came to Ploegsteert on April 3rd, and celebrated Holy Communion for the Battalion on Easter Sunday. He also consecrated the Battalion's graveyard in the village.

His regret at not being allowed to see the members of the Battalion in the trenches was shared by all ranks.

April 17th. Two brigades had been withdrawn to the neighbourhood of Steenwerck by this date, and the 4th Division started its first period of rest since the Retreat.

April 24th. Orders were received on the 22nd for these brigades to be ready to move at an hour's notice. The London Rifle Brigade actually entrained at mid-day on the 24th, and spent the night in billets outside Poperinghe, moving off at 5.30 a.m. next morning to the outskirts of Vlamertinghe. It stopped there till 6 p.m., when it paraded with the rest of the Brigade (less the East Lancashires) to go into the Salient.

Second Battle of Ypres. Since the first gas attack on the evening of April 22nd, little definite information had been available as to the situation between the left of the 28th Division (some 1,000 yards N.N.E. of Zonnebeke) and along the whole north side of the Salient down to the canal near

Boesinghe. The Canadians had held on with the grimmest determination in the neighbourhood of St. Julian, while what became to be known as Geddes' force held the line from the canal up to the Canadians. Geddes' force consisted originally of the supports and reserves (isolated companies and battalions) from the south and east sides of the Salient. By the night of the 25th this force had been supplemented by the 10th Brigade, the Northumbrian Territorial Division, the Lahore Division, and the 13th Brigade from the 5th Division.

The 11th Brigade was ordered on this night **April 25th.** to join up the left of the 28th Division with the right of the 10th Brigade, and so relieve the Canadians, who were still holding out in the neighbourhood of St. Julian.

No information was forthcoming as to the location of either of these forces, and it would seem that, instead of one continuous line, there were many small parties holding out in isolated groups.

Two officers from each Battalion had been sent up in advance (Captain Husey and Lieutenant Johnston from the London Rifle Brigade), but no available information could be collected, except that there was apparently a gap.

That night the Hants joined up with the 28th Division, and prolonged the line nearly to the junction of the Zonnebeke-St. Julian and

c

Ypres-Passchendale roads. There was, however, still a gap of nearly 1,000 yards between its left and the rest of the Brigade which had prolonged the line from the right of the 10th Brigade and part of the Northumbrian Division.

The London Rifle Brigade, being in support, had been instructed to dig itself in 600 yards south-east of Fortuin.

April 26th. The Battalion did not reach this position until 1.45 a.m., but, thanks to an early morning mist, it was able to secure fairly good cover by daylight.

On this day, and daily for the next seven days, the Battalion was heavily shelled, and suffered a high percentage of casualties, chiefly from enfilade fire.

Orders were received for a company to move early in the afternoon and take up a position that would join up the gap existing between the Somerset Light Infantry and the Hants. "C" Company was detailed, but a personal reconnaissance by the Officer Commanding the Company (Major Burnell) convinced higher authority that it was not only impossible to move the men by day, but that the Hants' left could not be found. Orders were accordingly received for the whole Battalion to move at dusk into the gap. Moving by a somewhat circuitous route, it arrived at its position, and dug in for the second night in succession. Owing to the darkness, most, if

To face page 18.

BATTALION HEADQUARTERS.
11*th May*, 1915.

To face page 19.

YSER CANAL.

not all, of the rules as to "artillery formation" were of necessity transgressed on this occasion.

The left of its line joined the Somersets, and the right an isolated party on the Zonnebeke-St. Julian road, which was supporting the Hants' left some 500 yards further forward to the right front.

It was not until this night that the Rifle Brigade finally dug across and joined up with the Hants, so that there was once more a continuous line. *April 28th.*

The London Rifle Brigade, having now become the second line, was moved up on this night to relieve the 4th East Yorks. The latter, with the 4th Yorks, were split up among the Battalions of the 11th Brigade, two companies of the latter being attached to the London Rifle Brigade. (The East Lancs had rejoined the Brigade by this time.) *April 29th.*

About 5 p.m., under cover of very heavy shell fire and gas, the Germans advanced from the ridge beyond the Haanebeke stream into the dead ground on the near side of the stream, where they dug in some 300 yards away, though on the left they got up much closer under cover of the houses. *May 2nd.*

The London Rifle Brigade casualties were very heavy, especially on the right, where the ground was more open.

Though the Battalion was affected by the gas for about 10 minutes, there was sufficient wind to dissipate it before any serious damage was done.

There is no doubt that, during their advance from about 1,000 yards till they got into dead ground, the Germans suffered fairly heavy casualties from the rifle fire of the two companies on the right, and this may possibly have deterred them from trying to leave the dead ground. With the assistance of the two companies of the 4th Yorks and one company of the East Lancs, which was also attached to the Battalion, the damage to the trenches was almost all repaired during the night, and all the wounded were evacuated.

May 3rd. On this night the line was readjusted, and the whole Brigade retired through the new line in rear without a single casualty.

May 4th. The actual withdrawal commenced at 12.45 a.m., commencing from the right of Battalions. Wieltje was timed to be reached at 1.45 a.m.

The casualties over the period April 25th to May 4th were 16 officers and 392 other ranks.

May 4th— 8th. These days were spent at various places in the woods behind Vlamertinghe resting, reorganising, and dealing with accumulations of mail.

May 9th. The Battalion moved early in the morning to the grounds of the Chateau at Vlamertinghe. On this night and the next one it had to dig on

To face page 20.

MAJOR A. S. BATES.
20th May, 1915.

To face page 21.

OFFICERS.
20th May, 1915.

the east side of the canal on the north of La Brique.

The Battalion moved up to the canal bank, **May 11th.** and occupied some very insanitary dug-outs, which had not been previously inhabited by British troops.

The London Rifle Brigade took over from the **May 12th.** Dublins a section of the front line, and was on the extreme right of the 4th Division. A Cavalry Division was on its immediate right.

Extract from Sir John French's despatch:— **May 13th.**
"On the 13th May the heaviest bombardment yet experienced broke out at 4.30 a.m., and continued with little intermission throughout the day. . . . The 5th London Regiment, despite very heavy casualties, maintained their position unfalteringly."

Extract from John Buchan's "History of the War," Vol. VII.:—

"Early in the morning of Thursday, May 13th, a day of biting north winds and drenching rains, a terrific bombardment began. . . . The infantry on the left of the cavalry were fiercely attacked, but contrived to hold their own. . . . The London Rifle Brigade had lost most of its men in the earlier fighting. It began the day 278 strong, and before evening 91 more had gone. One piece of breastwork was held by Sergeant Douglas Belcher with four survivors and two Hussars, whom he had picked up, and though the trench was blown in, and the Germans attacked with their infantry, he succeeded in bluffing the enemy by rapid fire, and holding the ground until relief came. That gallant stand, for which the Victoria Cross was awarded, saved the right of the 4th Division. . . ."

"A" and part of "B" Companies were in the front line. "C" Company garrisoned three fortified supporting points. The rest of "B" Company and "D" were in support. The reinforcement of the front line commenced at about 8 a.m. (the shelling on the Battalion's sector had started at 4 a.m.). The distance between the front line and the supports was about 900 yards.

The shelling did not cease till 6 p.m. Later in the evening the Battalion was withdrawn to the second line.

Captain Oppenheim, D.S.O., was wounded on this date, and Lieutenant H. L. Johnston took over the duties of Adjutant. He was subsequently confirmed in the appointment, and held it till April 7th, 1916, when he took over command of a company, being succeeded by Captain F. H. Wallis.

May 14th. This evening the Battalion moved into the trenches in front of La Brique, which it had dug less than a week before.

May 15th. The Battalion moved further forward into the second line, and two companies of the 6th Bat-

To face page 22.

LIEUT. TREVELYAN AND " A " COMPANY.
20th May, 1915.

To face page 23.

CAPTAIN OTTER AND " B " COMPANY.
20*th May,* 1915.

talion Northumberland Fusiliers were attached to it.

The Battalion was withdrawn to the canal bank. **May 16th.**

Orders were received that the London Rifle Brigade was to be withdrawn and sent the next day to General Headquarters. The Battalion marched that evening to Vlamertinghe, and was billeted there. **May 19th.**

The Battalion marched past the Divisional Commander after he had inspected it, and expressed his deep appreciation of all it had done since April 25th. It boarded the motor-buses, and proceeded to General Headquarters. **May 20th.**

The London Rifle Brigade thus left the 4th Division after six months.

The Brigade, Divisional, and Corps Commanders had all personally thanked the Battalion for the work it had done, and congratulated it on its behaviour under the most trying circumstances. But perhaps even more valued were the farewell letters from the Battalions of the 11th Brigade, showing, as they did, that they really felt the London Rifle Brigade to have become part of their Regular Brigade.

The London Rifle Brigade arrived at Tatinghem, and enjoyed ten days' complete rest during perfect weather.

The Rangers and Kensingtons had also been withdrawn from the line.

June 1st. These three Battalions were amalgamated for work on lines of communications. This entailed the handing over of all the active service equipment, and also all transport. The latter was a bitter blow, as the work of the transport, personnel, and animals had been beyond all praise. It is worth noting that in spite of the very heavy work of the previous four weeks the transport had actually accomplished the thirty-mile trek from the Salient in under 20 hours.

**Lines of Communication.
June 1st—Oct. 1st.** This period calls for no detailed treatment. Headquarters, and the balance of the men not employed at the different railheads, remained at St. Omer, first in the artillery barracks, and from July 1st under canvas.

The numbers at the various railheads altered very considerably from time to time, e.g., on June 6th 210 other ranks were scattered over fifteen stations, and on September 24th there were 374 other ranks at twenty-one different stations.

In addition to these details, the Battalion was called upon to furnish escorts and large parties for detraining work.

During the battle of Loos the Kensingtons and London Rifle Brigade between them furnished all the escorts for German prisoners, every available man, including grooms and officers' servants, being used.

The variety of the work on lines of communication provided scope for every type of

SEC.-LIEUT. F. D. CHARLES AND "C" COMPANY.
20th May, 1915.

To face page 25.

SEC.-LIEUT. WALLIS AND "D" COMPANY.
20th May, 1915.

individual—clerks to R.T.O.'s, telephone operators, guards, shell fuse setters, navvies on coal wharves, caretakers of a horse rest camp, hospital orderlies—while from time to time at small stations non-commissioned officers were left in complete charge.

From September 2nd to 30th the following four officers were lent to the Gas Brigade, and took part in the battle of Loos:—Captain R. E. Otter, Lieutenant F. H. Wallis, and Sec.-Lieutenants A. B. White and F. D. Charles.

On August 9th the composite Battalion was broken up, and each unit regained its individuality. This did not make any practical difference until October 2nd, when the London Rifle Brigade was transferred from the lines of communication to General Headquarters troops, and marched to Blendecques, the band of the Artists being kindly lent by their Commanding Officer to play it out.

While the Battalion was under canvas at General Headquarters, the officers messed in the Salle d'Honneur of the 8th Regiment of Infantry. On leaving, a present of a glass inkpot, with the regimental crest of the London Rifle Brigade, was sent to this French regiment as a small memento of the occasion. A most cordial and charming reply was received by Colonel Bates from Colonel Roubert, in which the latter looked forward to seeing the London Rifle Brigade once again in his barracks after victory had crowned the Allies' arms.

Oct. 2nd—25th.   The stay at Blendecques was intended to be a period of training before being sent back to the front. The actual period was 23 days, but, as it took more than a week to collect all the details from the various railheads, little more than a fortnight's full training was possible.

The reluctance of the authorities at these railheads to part with their London Rifle Brigade detachments, even after their reliefs had arrived, although complimentary, was not a little annoying, but the grateful letters received by the Commanding Officer in some measure compensated for the delay.

These three weeks were a period of re-mobilisation. Most of the non-commissioned officers who had survived Ypres had taken commissions. All the specialists had to be retrained. The transport and detailed equipment had to be indented for. The essentials were received by degrees, and actually completed a few days before the Battalion moved.

Oct. 25th.   The London Rifle Brigade moved by motor-bus in pouring rain to join the 3rd Division, which was resting east of Cassel. It relieved the Honourable Artillery Company in the 8th Infantry Brigade. The latter Battalion returned in the same buses. The transport had marched on the previous day.

Incessant rain and frequent inspections, combined with training on the lines laid down by the new Division, employed the time up to November 23rd.

To face page 26.

SEC.-LIEUT. BARKER AND M.G. TEAM.
20*th May*, 1915.

To face page 27.

THE BARRACKS, GENERAL HEADQUARTERS.

The Battalion marched to Poperinghe. For **Nov. 23rd.**
the first time it now had a bombing section of
2 officers and 70 other ranks; a sniping detachment was also organised.

The Battalion relieved the Liverpool Scottish **Nov. 29th.**
in the front line. The trenches were in a
desperate state, with very few traverses, no
complete communication trenches or second
line, and mud quite indescribable. They were
also overlooked, and enfiladed by the enemy.
The tour was normally seven days, with two
companies in the front line and two in reserve
near Battalion Headquarters.

Work was rendered very difficult owing to the
water-logged nature of the ground.

Ration parties took as much as seven hours to
accomplish one round journey.

On the whole, the Battalion was amazingly
fortunate while in these trenches. It suffered
casualties from occasional shelling and sniping,
but on certainly two occasions the enemy
bombarded the trenches and blew in fifty yards
of parapet without inflicting a single casualty.

The march to and from the trenches was an
exceedingly trying one. Only once was part of
the Battalion able to use motor-buses, but, after
the first tour, use was made of the " Ypres Express," to whose Commanding Officer the London Rifle Brigade will ever remain indebted.

The Battalion was in the trenches during the
abortive gas attack on December 19th, but was

not affected by the gas, which passed just behind it.

Christmas Day was spent in Poperinghe.

1916.
Jan. 4th. On leaving the trenches on this date the Battalion was kept in Brigade reserve. Apart from heavy night-working parties, the week was not too uncomfortable, though baths were impossible.

Jan. 18th. The London Rifle Brigade returned to rest under canvas instead of to billets.

Feb. 1—8. Owing to the relief of the 3rd Division this period was one of variety. The Battalion marched from trenches to rest, and back into reserve. It was attached to three different Brigades, and for a time was Divisional Troops. Eventually, on the 8th, orders were received to entrain the next day. The various outlying details were collected before midnight.

Feb. 9th. The Battalion entrained for the South.

Gommecourt. July 1st. This fighting is too recent for any details, however bare, to be given.

Previous to this date the Battalion, now part of as fine a Territorial Division as France had ever seen, took its ordinary tour of training and trenches. It was, of course, known that the Division was going "over the top" at the beginning of the offensive, and all training was carried out with this great end in view.

The following extract from the account published in the Press is given here, not because the

POPERINGHE, 1915.

VOORMEZEELE CHURCH.

writer of these notes does not feel able to give his own account, but because he might unwittingly say more than the Censor would feel able to pass :—

"I am about to give, on first-hand information, an account of the part which has been played by certain of our famous London Regiments. These regiments, which included the London Rifle Brigade, the Queen Victoria's Rifles, the Rangers, the Queen's Westminsters, and London Scottish, had assigned to them certain objectives near Gommecourt, towards the northern end of our original line of advance, where, as is well known, owing to the extraordinary preparations which the enemy had made in that direction, we did not fare so well as we have done, and continue to do, further south. The London Regiments, which fought with magnificent gallantry and tenacity, did, in fact, accomplish their primary objects, but, owing to circumstances beyond their control, they subsequently had to retire to a line which nearly corresponds to that they occupied before the battle began. . . ."

For its work on this day the Corps, of which the Division formed a part, received a special verbal message of thanks, delivered by one of Sir Douglas Haig's A.D.C.'s. This was subsequently confirmed in writing by the Chief of the General Staff.

Lieut.-Colonel Bates, D.S.O., was given sick leave in August, and Major R. H. Husey, M.C., took command. Under his leadership the Battalion added to its laurels in the fighting during September.

SECOND BATTALION.

At the beginning of September, 1914, permission was obtained to form a second Battalion. Recruiting was commenced at Headquarters in Bunhill Row on the 3rd, and the Battalion was filled in one day. So great was the rush of recruits that, had it been possible to obtain leave to do so, another Battalion could easily have been formed. Great care was taken, under these advantageous circumstances, in the selection of recruits. Those taken, combined with the draft from the 1st Battalion of men who were unable at that time to undertake the foreign service obligation, made up a fine Battalion.

Of the officers on formation, the following had formerly served in the Regiment, or were serving, and transferred from the 1st Battalion under the home service condition :—

> Lieut.-Colonel G. R. Tod, formerly Adjutant for five years, 1898-1903.
> Major G. Harvest.
> Quartermaster and Hon. Major J. Guppy.

To face page 30.

TRENCH BATTALION HEADQUARTERS.
November, 1915—February, 1916.

To face page 31.

ENTRANCE TO CAMP, REST BILLETS, MAY, 1916, WHERE THE LORD MAYOR SAW THE BATTALION ON PARADE.

Captain C. G. H. Macgill, M.V.O., who acted as Adjutant until the formation of the Home Service Provisional Battalion.
Captain S. Bowers.
Captain C. R. Bland.
Captain H. B. Prior.
Captain C. E. Johnstone.
Captain C. Furze.
Lieutenant B. E. Bland.

THIRD BATTALION.

The 3rd Battalion was raised on November 30th, 1914. The first Commanding Officer was Colonel H. C. Cholmondeley, C.B. (see pages 3 and 4). The Battalion was fortunate in having the help of several old members of the Regiment in the commissioned and non-commissioned ranks. They were invaluable in carrying on to the new men the traditions and ésprit de corps of the London Rifle Brigade.

After some five months in London, the Battalion proceeded at the end of April by train to Wimbledon, and on, by route march, to Tadworth, where it went under canvas. Soon after its arrival Colonel Cholmondeley was given command of a 4th Line Brigade, and the command of the Battalion was taken over by Major Norman C. King, T.D., who went out to the front with the 1st Battalion, and had been invalided home. Lieut.-Colonel King, being the officer with the senior permanent rank on the cadre of the Regiment, now commands it.

The system of training adopted was that of a public school; that is to say, the company represented the house, and the Captain the house master, who administered the company, but was not responsible for its training. The instructors in each subject—e.g., drill, musketry, bombing, etc.—each had their own staff of assistants, and every platoon was taken up in turn for its lesson. This represented the forms of a school. The system proved very successful, and received commendation from high authority. It was subsequently recommended for adoption over the whole of the Southern Command, but was too much of a departure from tradition to be taken over as it stood, though it was recommended in a modified form.

As the summer of 1915 passed on, officers from the 1st Battalion, who had been wounded in the second battle of Ypres in April-May, were posted to the 3rd Battalion on recovery. Thus began the circulation between the 1st and 3rd Battalions which has proved so invaluable in keeping close touch and sympathy between those at the front and those at home.

On November 12th the Battalion moved to billets in Sutton, and received the greatest kindness and consideration there. Everything possible was done for the comfort of the Battalion, and not the least of the kindnesses received were the services at Christchurch, under the Rev. Courtney Gale. Nothing could have exceeded the warmth and vigour of the church parades, which were much appreciated by all ranks.

On January 10th, 1916, the Battalion moved to its present camp.

ADMINISTRATIVE CENTRE.

The Headquarters and Depôt or Administrative Centre are situated at 130, Bunhill Row, E.C., and are in charge of Captain H. Ferguson, to whom the Regiment owes a considerable debt of gratitude for the whole-hearted way he has thrown himself into the work since he joined. Having been private secretary to the late Lord Roberts, he has brought a ripe knowledge and warm appreciation of the Territorial Force to bear on the thousand and one details which have to be arranged from Headquarters. Here it is that recruits receive their equipment and their first insight into drill.

The finances of the Regiment since war broke out have been ably looked after by Major C. W. Cornish, V.D., who took up the reins again after having laid them down in 1908.

The London Rifle Brigade Mutual Aid Society centres in Bunhill Row, and a copy of its scheme is given in Appendix F.

The Prisoners' Aid Fund, for sending food and warm clothing to non-commissioned officers and riflemen of the Regiment who are prisoners, is also controlled from Headquarters. Weekly parcels are sent by ladies of the Regiment to any whose relatives are not in a position to send them all they require.

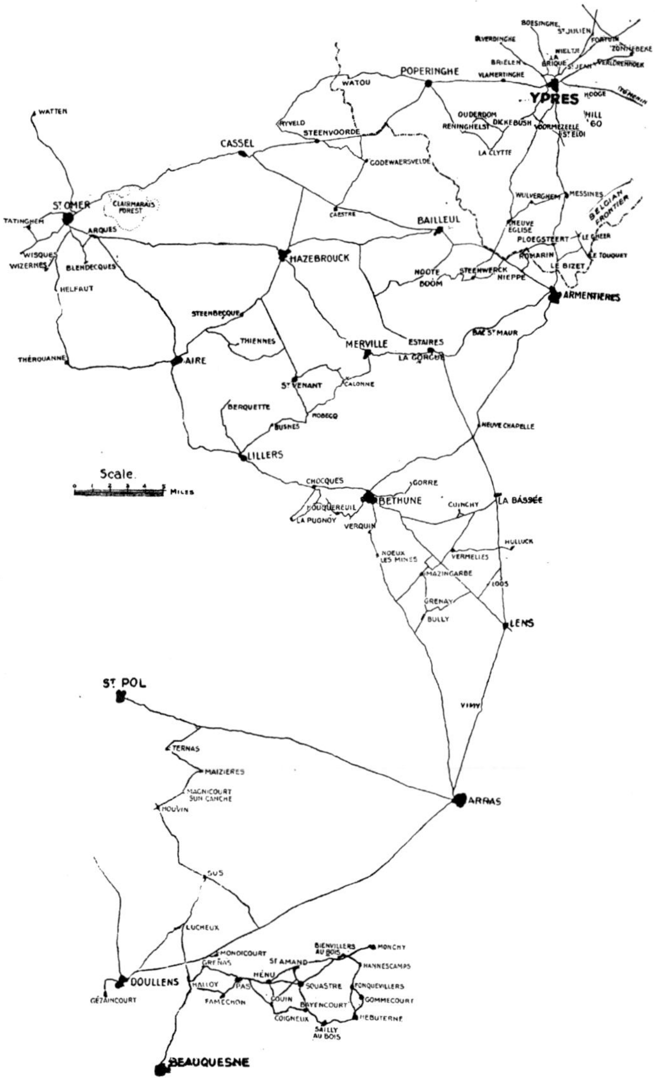

BOESINGHE
ST JULIEN
FORTUIN
ZONNEBEKE
ELVERDINGHE
WIELTJE
LA BRIQUE
BRIELEN
ST JEAN
VERLORENHOEK
POPERINGHE
VLAMERTINGHE
WATOU
YPRES
HOOGE
TO MENIN
HILL 60
WATTEN
OUDERDOM
RENINGHELST
DICKEBUSH
VOORMEZEELE
ST ELOI
RYVELD
STEENVOORDE
LA CLYTTE
CASSEL
GODEWAERSVELDE
WULVERGHEM
MESSINES
BELGIAN FRONTIER
ST OMER
CLAIRMARAIS FOREST
CAESTRE
BAILLEUL
NEUVE EGLISE
TATINGHEM
ARQUES
PLOEGSTEERT
LE GHEER
ROMARIN
LE TOUQUET
WISQUES
HAZEBROUCK
WIZERNES
BLENDECQUES
NOOTE BOOM
STEENWERCK
NIEPPE
LE BIZET
HELFAUT
ARMENTIERES
STEENBECQUE
THIENNES
BAC ST MAUR
MERVILLE
ESTAIRES
THÉROUANNE
AIRE
LA GORGUE
ST VENANT
CALONNE
BERQUETTE
ROBECQ
BUSNES
NEUVE CHAPELLE
LILLERS
Scale.
0 1 2 3 4 5 MILES
CHOCQUES
GORRE
BETHUNE
LA BASSÉE
FOUQUEREUIL
CUINCHY
LA PUGNOY
VERQUIN
HULLUCK
NOEUX LES MINES
VERMELLES
MAZINGARBE
LOOS
GRENAY
BULLY
LENS
ST POL
VIMY
TERNAS
MAIZIERES
MAGNICOURT SUR CANCHE
HOUVIN
ARRAS
SUS
LUCHEUX
BIENVILLERS AU BOIS
MONCHY
MONDICOURT
ST AMAND
HANNESCAMPS
GREÑAS
HÉNU
DOULLENS
HALLOY
PAS
SOUASTRE
FONQUEVILLERS
GÉZAINCOURT
FAMECHON
COUIN
BAYENCOURT
GOMMECOURT
COIGNEUX
HÉBUTERNE
SAILLY AU BOIS
BEAUQUESNE

APPENDIX A.

HONOURS AND REWARDS.

Victoria Cross.

9539 Lance-Sergeant Douglas Walter Belcher (now Sec.-Lieutenant, Queen Victoria's Rifles).

K.C.V.O.

The Bishop of London.

C.M.G.

Lieut.-Colonel W. D. The Earl Cairns.

D.S.O.

Major A. S. Bates.
Captain A. C. Oppenheim, King's Royal Rifle Corps.

Military Cross (10).

Captain R. H. Husey.
Captain J. R. Somers-Smith.
Captain H. L. Johnston.
Captain C. W. Trevelyan.
Captain F. H. Wallis.
Captain R. Russell.
Captain F. H. Crews.
Lieutenant E. R. Williamson (with a Trench Mortar Battery).
Sec.-Lieutenant A. K. Dodds (attached 181st Company, Royal Engineers).
Sec.-Lieutenant R. E. Petley.

D.C.M. (12).

9338 Sergeant (now Captain, Hampshire R., T.F.) W. F. Pothecary.
6968 Signalling Sergeant E. A. Adams.
8541 Sergeant R. V. Todd.
9435 Transport Sergeant A. Gordon (now Sec.-Lieutenant, London Rifle Brigade).
515 Sergeant W. M. Lilley.
9996 Sergeant W. A. Roulston (killed).
9497 Corporal (now Lieutenant, London Rifle Brigade) G. G. Boston.
75 Lance-Corporal T. H. Stratsom (now Sec.-Lieutenant, London Rifle Brigade).
11003 Lance-Corporal C. Taylor.
1006 Rifleman J. S. Lindsay (now Sec.-Lieutenant, London Rifle Brigade).
8896 Rifleman R. S. Clark.
10839 Rifleman E. L. Kench.

Military Medal (28).

1867 Regimental Sergeant-Major J. Adams.
660 Sergeant (now Sec.-Lieutenant, London Rifle Brigade) P. T. Dyer.
10835 Sergeant F. C. Keele.
9412 Sergeant (now Sec.-Lieutenant, London Rifle Brigade) E. H. Slade.
1131 Sergeant W. G. T. Mason.
776 Corporal R. F. Ebbetts.
9535 Corporal (now Sec.-Lieutenant, Lincolnshire Regiment) P. Godsmark.
9921 Lce.-Cpl. (now Sergeant) L. W. Billington.

9289 Lance-Corporal (now Sec.-Lieutenant, London Rifle Brigade) H. J. F. Crisp.
1621 Lance-Corporal J. H. Foaden.
1220 Lance-Corporal (now at Officers' Cadet School) V. L. A. Fowle.
9899 Lance-Corporal J. O. Haylock (now Sergeant-Dispenser, Northumbrian Field Ambulance).
9471 Lance-Corporal (now Sec.-Lieutenant, Cheshire Regiment) H. J. C. Rowe.
9137 Lance-Corporal (now Sec.-Lieutenant, King's Own Royal Lancaster Regiment) R. H. Stonnill.
9453 Lance-Corporal (now Corporal) H. Turner.
762 Lance-Corporal R. E. Parslow.
787 Sergeant C. W. Bradford (killed).
1124 Rifleman H. G. Buck.
1289 Rifleman F. A. Crocker.
92 Rifleman (now Sec.-Lieutenant, Royal Field Artillery) W. E. Dunnett.
2516 Rifleman H. W. Dunk.
2822 Rifleman A. F. H. Edington.
9457 Rifleman (now Sec.-Lieutenant, London Regiment) G. Gordon.
10535 Rifleman W. Hawthorn.
161 Rifleman (now Sec.-Lieutenant, London Regiment) E. W. G. Hodgkinson.
9609 Rifleman (now Sec.-Lieutenant, London Regiment) E. B. Latham.
9597 Rifleman (now Sec.-Lieutenant, London Regiment) W. E. Lockhart.
147 Rifleman (Sec.-Lieutenant, Oxford and Bucks Light Infantry) A. C. Thomas (killed).

Croix de Guerre (with palm leaves).

515 Sergeant W. M. Lilley.

All above Orders, Decorations, and Medals were won by officers, non-commissioned officers, and riflemen while serving with, or wearing the uniform of, the Regiment.

The following officers, who served with or in the ranks of the 1st Battalion, London Rifle Brigade, have gained the award shown after their names since being transferred, or commissioned, to other Regiments* : —

Sec.-Lieutenant H. H. Linzell, The Border Regiment, Military Cross.
Sec.-Lieutenant D. Blofeld, The London Regiment, Military Cross (killed).
Sec.-Lieutenant S. R. Hogg, Royal Fusiliers, Military Cross.

---

* This list does not claim to be complete. Any additions should be sent to the Officer in Charge Depôt, where a record will be kept.

APPENDIX B.

The following officers and other ranks have been mentioned in despatches:—

Lieut.-Colonel W. D. Earl Cairns.
The Bishop of London.
Lieut.-Colonel A. S. Bates (3).
Major A. D. Ducat, M.B., T.D., R.A.M.C. (T.F.).
Captain A. C. Oppenheim, King's Royal Rifle Corps (2).
Captain R. H. Husey.
Captain J. R. Somers-Smith.
Captain C. W. Trevelyan.
Lieutenant R. Russell.
Sec.-Lieutenant W. L. Willett.
Sec.-Lieutenant A. K. Dodds.
709 Company Sergeant-Major A. J. R. Macveagh.
8488 Company Sergeant-Major (now Sec.-Lieutenant, Royal Field Artillery) B. K. Manbey.
8929 Corporal (now Sec.-Lieutenant, King's Royal Rifle Corps) T. H. Jenkin.
9391 Rifleman R. E. Peck.

The following officer who served in the ranks of the 1st Battalion, London Rifle Brigade, has also been mentioned in despatches since being commissioned to another regiment[*]:—

Temporary Sec.-Lieutenant L. E. Schultz, Wiltshire Regiment (killed).

---

[*] This list does not claim to be complete. Any additions should be sent to the Officer in Charge Depôt, where a record will be kept.

APPENDIX C.

Alphabetical list, by ranks—the latter as on 15/8/16—of London Rifle Brigade officers with service in France up to that date, excluding those now serving whose names have not been passed by the Censor for publication:—

Lieutenant-Colonels.

Name.	Joined B.E.F. as an Officer.	Left B.E.F.	
Bates, A. S.	5/11/14	15/8/16	
Cairns, W. D., Earl	5/11/14	9/4/15	
King, N. C.	5/11/14	6/1/15	
Matthey, C. G. R.	5/11/14	12/1/15	

Majors.

Burnell, C. D.	5/11/14	7/5/15	Wounded
MacGeagh, H. D. F.	5/11/14	13/1/15	
	31/8/15	3/12/15	
Soames, M. H.	5/11/14	17/7/15	

Captains.

Alcock, J. E.	20/12/14	21/2/15	Wounded
Bland, B. E.	23/12/14	9/3/15	
Charles, F. D.	8/5/15	16/9/16	Wounded
Charles, R. D. S.	19/2/15	7/5/15	Wounded
Cholmeley, G. H.	5/11/14	21/2/15	
	18/7/15	-/7/16	Wounded

Name.	Joined B.E.F. as an Officer.	Left B.E.F.	
de Cologan, A. T. B.	18/7/15	1/7/16	Prisoner
Harvey, B. S.	20/12/14	3/5/15	Wounded
	5/8/15	1/7/16	Killed
Johnston, H. L. ...	5/11/14	23/6/16	Wounded
Kirby, A. G.	5/11/14	20/12/14	Wounded
Kitching, G. C. ...	5/11/14	17/2/15	
Large, E. L.	5/11/14	21/5/15	Died of wounds
Lintott, A. L.	5/11/14	20/1/15	
	21/5/15	19/11/15	
Morrison, G. H. ...	5/11/14	31/3/15	Killed
Nobbs, H. G.	8/8/16	9/9/16	Wounded & Prisoner
Robinson, J. G. ...	5/11/14	25/1/16	
Russell, R.	11/2/15	21/4/16	
Somers-Smith, J. R.	5/11/14	3/6/15	
	24/10/15	1/7/16	Killed
White, A. B.	19/2/15	7/5/15	Wounded
	18/7/15	20/11/15	
Wills, E. C.	8/5/15	13/10/16	Wounded

Lieutenants.

Bantoft, E. S.	5/7/16	11/9/16	Died of wounds
Beard, H. C.	18/3/15	3/5/15	Wounded
Boston, G. G.	8/5/15	27/7/16	Wounded
Bromiley, B.	24/12/15	5/7/16	
Cartwright, G. H. G. M.	5/11/14	11/5/15	Wounded
Clode-Baker, G. E.	24/12/15	1/7/16	Killed

Name.	Joined B.E.F. as an Officer.	Left B.E.F.	
Dodds, A. K.	28/2/15	11/10/15	Gassed
Flindt, R. E. H.	11/2/15	7/5/15	Wounded
Fursdon, G. E. S.	5/11/14	2/5/15	Wounded
	18/7/15	4/9/15	
Long, C. W.	27/5/16	27/7/16	
Maynard, M. J.	8/5/15	–/10/16	Missing
Oldfield, P. B. B.	1/5/15	27/7/16	Wounded
Petersen, J. R. S.	5/11/14	5/5/16	
Pocock, B. L. E.	24/12/15	2/7/16	Wounded
Price, H. B.	5/11/14	3/5/15	Killed
Sedgwick, A. E.	26/2/15	6/5/15	Wounded
	12/8/16	10/9/16	Killed
Slessor, P.	5/11/14	22/12/14	
Titley, P.	19/1/16	26/6/16	
Vincent, H. G.	5/11/14	3/5/15	
Williamson, E. R.	24/12/15	10/9/16	Wounded & missing, believed killed
Wimble, A. S.	29/4/15	7/5/15	Wounded

Second-Lieutenants.

Appleton, E. R.	18/7/15	20/12/15	
Aste, P. J.	18/7/15	4/2/16	
Baldwin, N. E.	3/8/16	–/10/16	Wounded & missing
Balkwill, C. V.	27/5/16	1/7/16	Killed
Balls, F. A.	27/5/16	11/7/16	
Barker, H. C.	29/4/15	22/1/16	
	28/3/16	24/4/16	
Benns, A. L.	5/3/16	1/7/16	Killed
Betts, A. W. T.	2/5/15	17/5/15	Wounded

Name.	Joined B.E.F. as an Officer.	Left B.E.F.	
Brodie, C. G.	18/7/15	15/9/15	
Camden, H. M.	11/1/16	9/2/16	
Carrier, J. R.	8/5/16	8/10/16	Killed
Collis, L. W.	2/8/16	20/9/16	
Cotter, G. H.	11/2/15	12/4/15	Killed
Crisp, H. J. F.	27/5/16	14/9/16	Wounded
Doust, C. B.	14/3/16	1/7/16	Killed
Dyer, P. T.	19/7/16	29/9/16	Wounded
Feast, A. C.	8/5/15	17/5/15	
Forbes, K.	5/11/14	10/2/15	Killed
Gardiner, W. E. M.	8/5/16	19/7/16	Killed
Gooding, H. R. W.	19/4/15	13/5/15	Killed
Hill, R. L.	13/8/15	6/6/16	
Hogg, S. R.	2/5/15	23/1/16	
Howe, G. H.	27/5/16	19/8/16	
Hewitt, F. E.	11/1/16	20/5/16	
Keddie, G. D. F.	1/5/15	7/6/15	
Lindsay, J. S.	19/7/16	30/9/16	Wounded
Lines, S. M.	8/5/15	13/5/15	Killed
Lintott, R.	29/4/15	3/5/15	Killed
Lydall, R. F.	9/6/16	1/7/16	Wounded
Moore, E. G.	19/7/16	17/9/16	Wounded
Petley, R. E.	27/5/16	1/7/16	Wounded
Pocock, B. E.	29/4/15	13/5/15	Missing, believed killed
Pogose, I. R.	27/7/15	2/7/16	Died of wounds
Pool, E. E.	11/1/16	9/5/16	
Prior, T. A.	5/3/16	19/5/16	
Radford, P. D.	19/7/16	21/9/16	Wounded
Rose, E. W.	22/7/15	1/7/16	Wounded

Name.	Joined B.E.F. as an Officer.	Left B.E.F.	
Rose, O. H.	27/5/16	18/6/16	
Sawbridge, B. F.	8/5/16	1/7/16	Wounded
Sell, C. H.	19/1/16	-/9/16	Wounded
Sharman, A. P.	19/7/16	11/9/16	Wounded
Smith, H.	19/1/16	1/7/16	Wounded
Stransom, J. H.	29/4/15	30/4/15	Wounded
Ticehurst, G. H.	4/6/16	26/9/16	Wounded
Thomas, E. G.	27/5/16	5/7/16	Wounded
Warner, A.	27/5/16	1/7/16	Killed
Wheatley, F. M.	11/1/16	14/2/16	Wounded
Whitehead, L. E.	19/4/15	2/5/15	Wounded
Willett, W. L.	5/11/14	13/12/14	Wounded
Wray, M.	8/5/15	4/6/15	

APPENDIX D.

List of attached officers who have served with the 1st Battalion, London Rifle Brigade, in France, excluding those now with it whose names have not been passed by the Censor for publication:—

Adjutant on Mobilisation.

Capt. A. C. Oppenheim, King's Royal Rifle Corps, wounded 13/5/15.

Medical Officers.

NAME & REGIMENT.	Joined Battn.	Left Battn.	
Maj. A. D. Ducat, M.D., T.D.	5/11/14	27/2/15	
Capt. L. Crombie	12/5/16	-/8/16	
Capt. J. M. Moyes	6/5/15	31/1/16	
Lieut. Edmunds ...	27/2/15	28/4/15	Wounded
Lt. D. T. C. Frew	3/2/16	12/5/16	
Lt. J. D. Marshall	31/1/16	3/2/16	

Second-Lieutenants. [*]

Cole, C. H.	14/7/16	4/10/16	Killed
Hughes, C. R.	14/7/16	17/9/16	Wounded
Matthews, H. L. L.	9/7/16	9/9/16	Killed
Newling, A. J.	14/7/16	7/10/16	
Sanderson, G. S.	14/7/16	21/7/16	Killed
Unwin, R. W.	14/7/16	-/10/16	Killed
Wilkins, J. W.	14/7/16	-/9/16	Wounded

[*] All 11th London.

APPENDIX E.

Commissions.

Since the 1st Battalion landed in France, 535 of its non-commissioned officers and men have received commissions.

The majority of these were sent to the Cadet School at General Headquarters or to England, while the balance, just over 200, obtained their commissions when at home sick or recovering from wounds. Out of this number 65 (21 of "A," 20 of "B," 15 of "C," and 9 of "D" Companies) have been given commissions in the Regiment, and 30 of these received them direct in the field in the 1st Battalion.

For a Regiment, whose 1st Battalion was fighting, the total given below is a proud achievement. It was always a wrench to part with candidates, but the figures prove that the strictures, often heard, that Commanding Officers refused to part with their best men were unfounded in the case of the London Rifle Brigade.

A few commissions were granted before the 1st Battalion went abroad, but no details are, at present, available.

	Commissioned or transferred to O.T.C's and Officer Cadet Battalions.
1st Battalion	535
2nd Battalion	122
3rd Battalion	51
Total	708

APPENDIX F.

THE LONDON RIFLE BRIGADE MUTUAL AID FUND.

Trustees.

Lieut.-Colonel Earl Waldegrave, P.C., V.D.
Lieut.-Colonel Earl Cairns, C.M.G.
The Bishop of London, P.C., K.C.V.O.

Committee.

Major C. W. Cornish, V.D., nominated by the Trustees.

W. J. M. Burton, Esq. (late London Rifle Brigade), nominated by the Trustees.

Newton Dunn, Esq. (late London Rifle Brigade), nominated by 1st Battalion.

Major C. R. Bland, nominated by 2nd Battalion.

Company Quartermaster-Sergeant F. H. Anderson, nominated by 3rd Battalion.

Under the above title a fund has been inaugurated with the object of helping officers, non-commissioned officers and men of the Regiment who may be in need of assistance owing to injuries or incapacity due to the war, or to aid their dependants.

The Fund is administered by a Committee of five members, two of whom have been nominated by the Trustees, and are old members of the Regiment, and one member for each of the three Battalions, to be nominated by the Officers Commanding.

Support will be gladly received from friends and members of the Regiment, and donations may be sent to Captain H. S. Ferguson at Headquarters, 130, Bunhill Row, who has kindly consented to act as honorary secretary and treasurer to the Fund.